TABLE OF CONTENTS

ISBN 0-9747577-0-5

Editing and Cover Design
by David Farkas
inspirational speaker, writer and artist living in Amherst, MA.
He can be reached at 866-4-FARKAS
or dfarkas@farkas.com

About The Author

Jacki Rose has read, attended, and listened to over 100 self-help books, seminars, and audio programs.

This book is based on a program she gives titled: "Create the Live You Want."

Jacki has followed the steps in this book to create the life she wants. She is now living her passion of being a professional speaker and teaching others how to be great presenters.

To learn more about Jacki and her programs visit: www.JackiRose.com.

Introduction

Something Greater Is Out There For You!

Have you ever desperately wanted something that you did not get? Then, because you didn't get it, you got something even better?

When we don't get what we want we usually find something greater out there.

Several years ago I decided to pursue my dream. I dreamed of becoming a bicycle tour guide. I desperately wanted to spend my summer doing that, even though it didn't pay very much. I applied and actually got an interview. I was so excited! I drove five hours there and five hours back on the same day. The interview went great. I felt I would get the job. But I wouldn't find out until March, and this was January.

For two months I hoped and prayed I would be chosen. I started working out hard at the gym, taking spinning classes, which are very intense workouts on a stationery bike. All I thought about was getting that job and spending my summer doing what I love to do, bicycling.

What do you love to do? What if you could do it all summer long?

Finally, March came and I couldn't wait any longer. I called them up and asked "Did I get the job?!" I was expecting to hear, "Yes you did." But that's not what I heard. Instead I heard "You have not been chosen."

I was devastated. It seemed my dream was not going to come true after all. I felt rejected, disappointed, and sad. I needed to find something that would take the pain away.

No, I didn't reach for drugs, food or alcohol. Well, I may have had a cookie. But then I picked up one of my cycling magazines, and began searching. I didn't even know what I was searching for, but within seconds I found an ad for a bike trip across the country. I thought, "What the heck", "I'll just give them a call to see what it's all about." Three months later I was on an airplane to California to begin my cross country bike adventure.

Most people who know me know that I biked across the country, but what they don't know is how steep the hills were. They don't know how sick I got during the first couple of days from the high altitude

or how many saddle sores I got on my
derriere.

They also don't know about the incredible
people with whom I was so privileged to
ride. The man with one arm who was
riding a custom bike built just for him.
The young guy who, after a near fatal car
accident, was not expected to come out of
a coma, and certainly was not expected to
walk again. And, the 70-year-old women,
who was, 70 years old!

These amazing people were on my bike
trip across the country and I couldn't even
keep up with them!

On June 6, 1997, forty strangers from all
of the country, gathered together with a
common goal to ride their bikes from San
Francisco to New Hampshire in 52 days.

We began our journey leaving the Pacific Ocean by pedaling across San Francisco's Golden Gate Bridge and heading toward the deserts of Nevada. There we saw nothing for days, but after tackling the hills in Tahoe, we appreciated the flat terrain. Soon we were riding through the salty lakes of Utah, where we enjoyed views of the beautiful mountains.

Half way through the trip we arrived in Colorado where we caught glimpses of incredible mountain streams and peaceful green pastures until it was time for the most challenging climb of the trip. Monarch Pass is the continental divide between the Pacific and Atlantic Oceans. In just nine miles we climbed to an elevation of 11,312 feet! That would have been hard enough, but I had already acquired nasty, painful saddle sores.

I must admit, it was a very tough climb for me. Every now and then, I had to get off my bike and walk because of the dreadful pain. I was the last one to the top, but I made it. I found the rest of the group waiting for me, and they had been waiting quite a while! I was greeted with cheering, clapping, and sounds of "Yeah Jacki!" I was filled with a tremendous feeling of accomplishment.

There were many more challenges and many more accomplishments. After each accomplishment I was astonished at what I was capable of. When I say accomplishments, I mean interminable hills and biting headwinds, but I never gave up.

The ride continued over the roller coaster roads of Kansas and Missouri. We would climb to the top of the one hill, and then enjoy a fun ride down. When we got to the bottom, it didn't even level out. We were immediately greeted with another climb and then another fun ride down. This went on for days.

In Indianapolis we had an opportunity to ride our bikes around the Indy 500 speedway and the Major Taylor Velodrome. What fun that was.

From Pennsylvania to New York we enjoyed the fresh sea breeze of Lake Erie. From New York to Massachusetts we were exhilarated by breathtaking views of the Berkshires although we had lots more climbing to do before the trip was over.

Finally, after 52 days, 3700 miles, and a weight loss of only ten pounds, we made it to the Atlantic Ocean in New Hampshire.

There we dipped our wheels in the ocean, congratulated each other and felt overwhelmed with emotion. Sadness because we knew we probably would never see each other again, and joy because we didn't have to get on our bikes the next day! We also felt elation because we had accomplished what we set out to accomplish. We had experienced things most people will never experience.

Have you ever desperately wanted something, but didn't get it? Then, because you didn't get it, you got something even better?

My dream was to become a bicycle tour guide. Instead, I rode my bike across the country. A dream I never thought possible, and a life changing experience.

The next time you don't get what you want; remember there is something much greater out there for you. What ever you wanted that you didn't get, freed you up to go after a greater something. And that greater something is waiting for you right now. Go out there and find it today. Something greater is out there.

Chapter 1
Who Are You Listening To?

Sometimes when you go after what you want, you don't get it. But the progress and work towards your original goal leads you to discover something even greater, something that you wanted even more, that you didn't even realize you wanted.

The steps laid out in this book are the steps that I took to put my life in the direction I wanted it to go. The tools are the same tools I used to create the life that I wanted. These tools have helped me to develop a mind of my own, to build confidence in myself, to listen to my own voice and to have the guts to go after exactly what I wanted.

Do you know what you want?

Have you been doing what other people want for you or want you to do? I had been listening to other people for so long that I didn't know how to listen to myself. I didn't even know that was an option. The people I listened to were the ones who loved me the most and the ones I loved. They were people who wanted the best for me.

Do you know where listening to them got me? Where has it gotten you? It led me to a place which was unsatisfying and unfulfilling. I wasn't living the life that was right for me. I had lost my true identity because I was listening to others instead of listening to myself.

Who are the people in your life that you've been listening to? Are they your parents, family, and friends? Why do you listen to them? Because they love you and want what's best for you. They also usually speak with confidence. We usually believe people who appear confident or speak with conviction. It seems as if they really know what is right.

The only person who knows what's best for you is you! You are the only one who knows your thoughts and feelings. You are with yourself 24 hours a day. Others are with you much less than that. You know yourself better than anyone.

This book will help you to get to know yourself even better. The more you know yourself, the more you will discover what you want and the more you will be able to create for yourself.

When I was growing up, I said that the last thing I would ever be when I grew up was a secretary. I wanted to be a psychologist, an artist, or a lawyer. But, my parents wanted to protect me and wanted to give me the best advice possible. They wanted to make sure I took the path that would make me the happiest.

So, when I told them I wanted to be a psychologist, they would say to me, "You don't want to listen to people's problems all day long, you will be depressed." They didn't want me to be depressed. When I told them I wanted to be an artist, they said, "You won't make money at being an artist". They didn't want me to be poor. When I told them I wanted to be a Lawyer, they said, "You'll have to go to school for a lot of years. You don't want to do that." So, I believed them.

Whenever they told me what I didn't want I believed them and thought that was what I didn't want. So, I lost my true identity. I lost my ability to think and trust myself.

My parents are very loving and protective people who gave me a wonderful upbringing. Throughout my life they have always been there for me and have always wanted the best for me. I share this with you, because I believe many people will identify with this. Whether it is parents, siblings, teachers, or friends they always want the best for you.

I have found that the majority of the people I come in contact with have been listening to other people. They are living their lives according to what others think, losing sight of what they really want. That is why you are reading this book. I am also sure that you have advised other people in the same way that you have been advised.

Maybe you are a parent, and tell your kids what you think they should do. Maybe you have advised your family, maybe even

your parents on what they should do. I
know I have. If you are married or in a
romantic relationship, I know you tell your
significant other what they should do.

I ended up going into the profession my
parents told me I should. The one
profession I swore I would never become, a
secretary. I went to school for secretarial
science. That's my degree.

A year out of school, on my own, working
as a secretary, I decided to get my Real
Estate License. Being on my own helped
me gain a sense of identity and realize that
I was a person with a brain just like
anyone else.

I began listening to my own voice and
began talking to myself saying things like:
"What makes my parents, friends, and
family so right? I can be right. I just need
to trust myself and have confidence that I

can make decisions for myself that are right."

By the way, my parents had encouraged me to become a secretary because they felt it would be an easy way to get my foot in the door, and then work my way up in a company. They were right. After working in Real Estate for almost a year, I got a call from my old boss, for whom I had previously worked as a secretary. She had a new job as a director at a hotel where I had always wanted to work. She was calling to offer me a secretarial job.

I accepted. Within a short period of time I was in a management position. While working as a Sales Manager in the hotel industry, I put my entrepreneurial spirit to work and started a singles club.

A few years later, I was a full time social director at an apartment complex where I was in charge of planning activities seven days a week. This included planning special events, running the fitness center and hiring and training staff to run the operations of the clubhouse.

My next job was leading the Children's Continuing Education and Enrichment Program for a school district with more than fourteen Elementary Schools. My responsibilities included hiring and training hundreds of instructors, deciding what courses to offer, and working closely with school principals and parents.

After so many different careers, as well as many part time jobs, I hit a pothole in my road. I was in a rut. I was no longer feeling challenged, but I didn't have enough confidence in myself to realize that I was capable of much more.

Even though I had been working in manager and director level positions, and getting wonderful accolades, I was held back by insecurities and low self esteem. I interpreted statements from others to mean that I had limited capabilities and that I wasn't a very bright person.

My brothers said things that made me feel dumb (as many siblings do and I'm sure I was the same to them) and my parents said things that made me feel crazy when I told them about business ideas that I had. I'm sure they didn't realize how their comments made me feel and I'm sure their intention was not to make me feel that way. I'm also sure they felt strongly that they were right in telling me what was in my best interest.

Look at how I interpreted their comments. It's not what we hear from others but what we interpret their comments to mean.

That is how the self-destruction of our self-esteem begins.

Because of my low self-esteem, I believed others were right and I was wrong. So, even as an adult, and an accomplished working woman, I still believed my brothers, my parents, and everyone else with whom I came in contact. I allowed other's negative comments to get in the way of my life's ambitions. As a result, I ended up with low self-esteem, depressed about being unfulfilled, and feeling empty inside.

It is said that one of the causes of depression is not being able to express yourself and utilize your best skills, whether you know what they are or not.

So, I went to work to discover what I wanted, and I mean real work.

I left my job to bike across the country. I knew if I told my parents I was going to do this, they would tell me I was crazy and talk me out of it. I was still very easily influenced by them. I faxed them a letter worded in such a way that they couldn't discourage me from doing something that I really wanted to do.

By the way, the few times that I have had the confidence to go after what "I" wanted to do, without listening to or caring about what others had to say, I had the most fun and felt the happiest and most accomplished. When I listened to myself and didn't allow anyone else to influence my decision I had the best relationship, the best vacation, and the best career that I have ever had.

The relationship was the most fun, most loving, and the longest I had ever had. The vacation was a bike trip through Ireland, which was an absolutely phenomenal experience. The career is the one I have now, living out my dream of being a motivational speaker.

Think about a time that you did what you really wanted to do and didn't let anyone stop you. How did you feel? Probably pretty terrific!

I thought the bike trip would clear my head and allow me to figure out what I wanted to do next. But it didn't. All I could think about was getting to my destination each day. We averaged 80 miles a day, sometimes 100.

When I got back I did temp work (my secretarial experience often comes in very handy) and met with a career counselor for eight weeks.

By the fourth week we had come to the conclusion that instead of continuing with the usual four additional weeks of counseling, I would immediately begin the process of opening my own dating agency. The decision was obvious, because throughout my adult life, while I worked on other jobs, I had started singles clubs on the side.

It all started in High School when I was called "the matchmaker" because I spent my free time fixing my girlfriends up with my guy friends. I also have an entrepreneurial spirit and enjoy planning and hosting social events.

The counselor urged me not to discuss my decision with my family, because I might be easily discouraged by their reaction. So, what did I do? I went to lunch with my brother and father.

They kept probing, asking me what was happening with the career counselor. I tried not to say anything, but I finally gave in and told them.

You can guess what happened next. At my next career counseling session, I said I'd like to continue the regular sequence of sessions rather than pursuing the dating agency idea. The Counselor asked, "What happened between last week and this week? You were so gung ho and excited about starting this business, and now you are not." I answered, "I had lunch with my brother and father".

I looked up to my father and brother. I felt they were extremely smart and knew much more than I did. I believed that because they were very successful businessmen, they must be right.

How many times have you given power to other people rather than yourself?

When the eight-week session was complete, I hadn't discovered anything that I was passionate about. Sure, I had lots of interests, and jobs I'd like to do, but nothing that I was excited about. Passion is what I was looking for. The more passionate we are about something, the more motivated we can become. Passion brings us happiness, fulfillment and success.

I went back to the Hotel Industry, to a job I'd done before. I was actually overqualified for the position I accepted. I soon felt I was not utilizing my full potential, and felt unfulfilled and depressed again.

When you listen to other voices more than your own voice you may end up unfulfilled and depressed. Maybe that's how you feel right now. There is hope. Read on to the next chapter.

Chapter 2
Passion Discovery

I knew there was something better out there for me. I knew there had to be a career that I could be passionate and excited about. I wanted to live an exciting and fulfilling life. I continued to work toward figuring it out.

I went to Toastmasters, a non-profit public speaking organization, and realized how much I enjoyed public speaking. Through journal writing, and using the steps in this book, I discovered that training people is also something I love to do and that public speaking is a great passion of mine.

The more I researched these areas, the more excited I got. More importantly, my confidence increased.

I made a decision to listen to the positive feedback I was getting from my co-workers, friends, and fellow Toastmasters. I started to ignore the negative feedback I got from anyone else.

Once I focused on the positives, and decided to **believe** the positives, my entire life changed. I began to believe I could accomplish more and I could find something greater out there for me. Whatever we believe comes true for us.

One night I had the privilege of hearing a speech by a well-known Toastmaster and Professional Speaker, the late David McIlhenny. He was a gem, a role model, a wonderful man. His topic was Taking Risks.

He explained how risk taking affects your advancement in life. He explained that people who don't take risks are actually taking a risk without realizing it. For example, some people stay at their jobs, for fear of taking a risk and moving on to another job.

Mr. McIlhenny suggested that staying in your current job IS taking a risk. Who knows what may happen to your position down the road or what may happen to you in that position. He explained the remarkable benefits of taking a risk. Even if you don't get what you want, or you fail, you still have a greater chance for growth than if you did not take any risk at all.

Taking risks increases your chances of getting what you want, growing personally and professionally, and achieving happiness and fulfillment.

His speech had a huge impact on me. The following day, I went to work and took a huge risk. I quit my job to pursue my dream of becoming a professional speaker and corporate trainer.

Within a few months I was employed as a corporate trainer and was offering public seminars. Just working toward your goals makes you feel happier and more fulfilled because you feel more in control of your life. You begin to see the light at the end of the tunnel. When you are working towards your goals, you have more energy, more motivation and more happiness.

I'm at a place in my life that I never thought possible and I'm moving toward an even better place. I have discovered that one of the best feelings to have is to **know** what you want.

It feels even better when you take action steps towards getting what you want. This book is going to help you get these wonderful feelings.

Chapter 3
The 3 Fs
Freedom, Fun, & Fulfillment

It took a long time for me to figure out what I really wanted. But once I began listening to my own voice, listening to positive comments from others, and reading self-help books, it became much easier. I was able to discover what I wanted. I developed belief within myself that I could have what I wanted. Then the energy and motivation to go after what I wanted came automatically.

In this book I have taken all that I've learned and condensed it into a quick and easy format so you can achieve the same things in your life.

This book is designed to help you move your life in the direction you want to go and achieve whatever you want.

I call it **the 3 F's: Freedom, Fun, And Fulfillment.**

Freedom: Our thoughts create our prison cells. How would you feel if anyone or anything that has kept you from getting what you want no longer had an influence on you? How would it feel to have total confidence in your own thoughts, ideas, and capabilities?

FREE!

Free from worrying about what others will say, do, or feel. Free to express yourself in the way you were meant to express yourself. Free to have the life you desire. What a great feeling!

Fun: Would you like to have more fun in your life? If you create the life you really want, do you think you would have more fun? Absolutely!

When you have fun, people around you also have fun because it's contagious. When you have fun, you are happier, more energetic, and more fulfilled. You are more likeable, a greater influence on others, and more productive. Fun gives you more energy. The more energy you have the more you can accomplish.

Fulfillment: Are you totally fulfilled right now so that you don't need or want anything else?

Probably not or you wouldn't be reading this book. But, because you are reading this book, you can learn to achieve total fulfillment.

The majority of people in this world are so trapped in their own limiting beliefs (their own prisons) that they don't even attempt to seek Fulfillment, Fun and Freedom. They miss out on what could have been. The fact that you have chosen to get this book, and actually read it, is a clear sign that you do not want to miss out.

If you could feel free to express yourself and live the life you want and if you had more fun in your life and felt totally fulfilled, living life to the fullest, not needing anything else, wouldn't you be truly happy and have everything you want?

Great! Then let's get started. There are 3 simple steps to achieving the 3 Fs of creating the life you want and living the life you were meant to live. They are to **KNOW** what you want, **BELIEVE** you can have it, and to take **ACTION** and make it happen.

Can you remember a time when you wanted more out of life, but you didn't know what you wanted and that kept you from getting more? How about a time you knew what you wanted, and you got it?

Stop reading and take a minute to really think of the answers to these two questions.

One day I decided to go out for a cup of coffee but didn't know where I wanted to go. I started from my suburban home driving west away from the city. I drove through several towns and passed several coffee shops, but just didn't know where I wanted to go. So I kept driving.

After heading west I somehow ended up going east, and into the city! I never go into the city! And when I do, I always get lost! I have no idea how I got there, and I still didn't know where I wanted to get that cup of coffee. But I DID know that I wanted to get out of the city and I believed I could get out.

I was out within minutes. Once I was out, I KNEW I wanted to go home, and in minutes I was home. When I arrived home, I realized I had driven in a huge circle. I ended up back where I started and had nothing to show for it. I never even got my cup of coffee.

When I didn't know where I wanted to get my cup of coffee, I didn't get my cup of coffee. You must know what you want in order to get it. If I knew where I wanted to go for that coffee, I would have driven in that direction and would have arrived there. Because I didn't know, I just kept driving. I ended up in a place I didn't want to be. Had I known exactly where I wanted to have that cup of coffee, I would have been able to drive in the right direction and would have had what I wanted in the first place, a cup of coffee.

Not knowing what you want can take you in a direction you really do not want to go. Once you know what you want, you can get there. You will get there.

A cup of coffee may seem inconsequential, but look what happened when I didn't know where I wanted to go to drink it. I ended up driving around for almost two hours. I was stuck in traffic in the city, a place I didn't want to be, and didn't feel comfortable. When I finally got home, I was exhausted.

No matter how big or how small the task, unless you know your destination, you just will not get there. In order to get what you want out of life, you must know what you want. Once you know what you want, you can move your life in the direction you want it to go. In the next chapter you will learn powerful ways to discover what you want.

Once you know what you want, you must believe that you can have it. This is the most crucial step. If you don't believe you can have it, you will never get it.

Henry Ford said, "Whether you think you can or you think you can't, you're right." I grew up reading the Little Engine that could "I think I can, I think I can, I KNOW I can". If you believed you could run a marathon, do you think you could run one? If you didn't think you could run a marathon, do you think you could run one?

We only accomplish what we believe we can accomplish. We only become who we believe we can become. Our thoughts create our lives. In this book I give you powerful tools to help you believe in yourself so that you can accomplish what you want to accomplish and become who you want to become.

Once you know what you want and believe you can have it, you must make it happen by taking action. This is quite obvious, isn't it? Unless you take action and make it happen, nothing will happen.

The keys to taking action are motivation, having enough energy, and knowing what to do.

As children many things are done for us and many things are beyond our control. When we become adults, many of us still allow others to control us. We don't end up with what we want, because we're waiting for it to happen, like it did when we were kids. But, other people aren't making things happen for us any more. For example, I remember wanting to go to Disney World as a child. Who made it happen? My parents did. Now if I wanted to go to Disney World and I called my parents to ask them to make it happen I doubt very much that they would pick up the phone, make my airline and hotel reservations, pick me up and drive me to the airport.

You know what? I don't even remember asking to go to Disney World as a child. It just happened. Mom and Dad told us we were going and that was it.

Life isn't that simple as adults, is it? Well, life is as simple or as difficult as we make it. Most of us are working hard. Are you working hard at what you want or what you don't want? I believe that when you work hard at what you want, life becomes easier and more joyful. Work towards the life you want and you have fun in the process.

When you are working toward your goals, you are happier. When you are happier, you have more energy. When you have more energy, you accomplish a lot more. So let's start having some fun and begin the process of living a more fulfilling life and feeling free to find something greater out there and to Take Your Life and Love It!

It is selfish *NOT* to take care of yourself.

The happier you are
The better person you become and
the better contributor you are to
society.

Chapter 4

What Do You Want?

Step #1 Discover What You Want

The first step in living a fulfilling life is to
know what you want. There are three ways
I recommend to help yourself discover
what you want. They are:

1. Spending Time Alone

2. Doing Something

3. Writing

Spending Time Alone
When you spend time with other people
you get to know them. When you spend
time with yourself you get to know
yourself.

I moved to California, by myself, for a
year. I got to know myself without even
trying. It was unavoidable. I came home

saying that it was the most worthwhile year of my life. By getting to know myself, I had developed a mind of my own and was not as easily influenced by others. I'm not suggesting that you just pick up and move away to be by yourself for a year. But I am suggesting that you arrange to spend time alone.

Even if it's only for five or ten minutes a day, those few minutes could be the most important time you spend. The more time you spend by yourself, the more you will know what you really want. When you know what you really want, you become happier instantly.

It's like solving a problem. How do you feel when you solve a problem? Less stressed? More focused? Relieved?

I find time to be by myself by walking, sitting by a quiet lake, or taking myself

out for lunch or coffee. I have found that
these activities create incredible thinking
power. When I walk, things sometimes
come to me in the first few minutes.
Go for a five-minute walk alone. You will
be amazed at what will come to mind. As a
bonus, taking a walk, sitting by a lake, or
drinking a nice warm cup of coffee or tea
will make you feel good. Go to a place that
makes you feel good. When you feel good,
your best thoughts tend to surface.

Doing Something
You can learn a lot just by doing
something. The more you do things the
more you will discover what's out there
and the more you will know what it feels
like. Unless you do it and feel it, you won't
know if it's really what you want.

For years I wanted to go parasailing. I
knew I would love it. I ached for it. While
vacationing in Hilton Head, I finally got an
opportunity to try it. I talked a friend into

going with me, in spite of her reluctance. She was sure she wouldn't like it. Finally she gave in to my begging and pleading.

We were on a boat with six other people. Four of them went before us. Then it was her turn. I was last. The first four had a wonderful time. As my friend watched each one, she became more excited about the adventure I had forced her into. It was finally her turn.

She was still a little frightened, but also a little excited. They buckled her up, and then raised her out. We watched her float high into the sky. She had a huge smile on her face and gave the signal to raise her even higher, which cost more. But she didn't care. She was having the time of her life! She didn't want to come back down.

But of course, she had to, because there was still one more person left to go. Me!

This was the moment I had been waiting for for years. I couldn't believe I was finally going to do what I've been dying to do for so long. I was so excited.

They buckled me up and raised me out. The moment I rose up, I felt sick! Seasickness, nausea, airsickness, motion sickness, whatever you want to call it, I had it. And, I had it bad! I wanted to come back down, but they couldn't hear me over the boat motor. I thought of signaling, but was afraid they would mistake it for a signal to raise me higher. I prayed that I just wouldn't vomit in front of everyone. I held on tight for the longest, most nauseous fifteen minutes of my life.

My friend didn't think she would like it, but she loved it. I thought I would love it, but I hated it. Unless you actually try something, you won't know if it's for you or not. Get out there and begin doing things. The more you do, the more you will discover what you like, what you don't like and, ultimately, what you want and who you are. The more you get to know yourself, the easier it is to uncover what you want.

Writing
Writing is an extremely powerful tool for discovering what you want. I can't emphasize this enough.

Writing clears your head. When your head is clear, you can think clearly. I would not be where I am today if I had not spent time writing. Here are specific writing exercises to help you clear your head, think clearly, and discover who you are and what you want. Each of us can achieve what we desire.

You may not desire something better because you just can't see yourself having it. That's because your mind is clogged with negativity, low self-esteem, and other people's opinions. You need to unclog your mind to think clearly.

What you want is already inside yourself. It may be deeply buried, but it's there. Once you get your thoughts out of your head and onto paper you can begin thinking with your heart. Your true desires are in your heart and in your gut, not in your head.

Before you can discover what you want, you need to know who you are. Once you know your identity, it is so much easier to figure out what you are meant to do. I suggest writing in a journal and re-writing the questions on the top of each page.

Writing exercise – **Who are you?**

A. Write the best memory or memories of your life. Think back to your childhood, and perhaps later in life. What was the best time or times of your life?

B. What were you doing?

C. Describe your personality and feelings at that time. How did you feel? How did you act? Who were you with? What did you like? etc.

D. If you could be any way you wanted to be how would you be? What characteristics would you have? Write it now in the present tense as if you are the way you would like to be. Write as many as you can.
Examples: *I am strong, ambitious, and successful, I am happy, I am patient, I am a*

dancer, I am an artist, I am a great lover, I am in love with a great person, I am a wonderful parent, I am a beautiful women, I am a charming man, I am an entrepreneur, I am a kind person, I am a funny guy who makes other people laugh, I am an athlete, I am a millionaire, I have lots of fun in my life"

E. Look at what you wrote. From that, come up with an identity statement. What you wrote is really who you are deep down inside. Think about who you truly are, and write an identity statement for yourself. Does it seem right to you? Does it tell who you really are? Does it excite you?

Examples: *I am a vibrant woman who enjoys being around children. I am an athlete who enjoys reading autobiographies of famous people. I am an artist who loves being around other people. I am a strong man living life to the fullest. I am genuine, patient, and fun to be around.*

It doesn't matter what you write or how you write it as long as it is written in a positive frame and in the present tense. Do not write anything like, *I am a lazy bum who just sits around and watches TV all day.* That is not who you ARE, even though it may be what you DO. You may do things that do not represent who you really are inside, because you haven't been in touch with, or have lost touch with who you really are. You are now getting back in touch. As you go throughout your day, repeat this statement to yourself over and over again.

Now that you are beginning to get to know yourself and are figuring out who you really are, you can start to figure out what you want. Here are two writing exercises to help you discover what you want.

Writing Exercise – What do you want?

A. List everything you want. At least 10 things, but aim for 20.

B. Circle your 5 favorite on your list.

C. Circle your 3 favorite things out of the 5 you circled in step B.

D. Put a huge star next to your most favorite thing out of the 3.

E. Rewrite your favorite things on a new sheet of paper.

F. List 10 to 20 ideas on how to get the thing you want most.

G. Circle your top 5, then top 3, then put a star next to your #1 favorite idea.

H. Take action on that one idea.

Writing Exercise – Zapped

If you could be zapped into the life of your dreams, what would that be? For this exercise, money is not an issue. Responsibility is not an issue. You have no memory of your current life and you now have a chance to have any life you want.

What would that be? What would your life look like if it were perfect? Write it down as if you are already living that life. In other words, write it in the present tense.

Example: *I am married to a loving spouse. We live in a beautiful house on the ocean. We own a sailboat. We have 3 children. We spend our time sailing, cycling, and spending quality time with our children. I have my own business as a consultant and earn $250,000 per year.* The more specific you can get the better.

Writing Exercise - **Realization**

Write down what you have discovered, learned, or became aware of through these exercises.

Writing is extremely powerful. It is the primary tool I used to discover what I wanted, to create belief in myself, and to figure out what steps I needed to take to make it all happen. I strongly recommend that you write on a regular basis. Get an attractive private journal. Go out of the house and find a nice quiet spot to write.

Discovering what you want is an ongoing journey. You will discover one thing that you want, which will lead to another thing that you want, which will lead to another and so on. Keep using these tools to discover what you want and you will get clearer and clearer about what you truly desire in your life.

It doesn't matter where you come from
It's where you're going

Don't do what's expected of you
You don't have to

Believe in yourself
Believe in yourself it's the key
Believe in yourself it's the key to all of your
dreams!

Chapter 5

You Can Have It

Step 2
Create belief within yourself that you can have what you want.

This is the biggie. It's the key. It is the key to making all your dreams come true.

As I mentioned earlier, I am a cyclist. One summer I signed up for a weeklong bike trip. I was out of work and didn't know what I wanted out of life. I wasn't very motivated to train for this ride, so when the time came, I didn't feel I was ready.

I considered canceling. But I talked myself out of canceling and into going. I was so glad I did. I had one of the best times of my life.

I took on the miles. I took on the hills. I took on the stormy weather. Call me crazy, but I loved it! I was so surprised and amazed with my capabilities that I was inspired to compose a song to describe how I was feeling and to describe a revelation that came to me.

Since we each rode at our own pace, and since I'm much slower than most, I rode alone a lot. That gave me lots of time to think. It also gave me an opportunity to sing out loud without anyone hearing me. The song goes like this:

It doesn't matter where you come from
It's where you're going
Don't do what's expected of you
You don't have to
Believe in yourself
Believe in yourself it's the key
Believe in yourself it's the key to all of your dreams
It doesn't matter where you come from
It's where you're going.

This truly is the biggie, the key. It is the
key to making all of your dreams come
true. You must believe in yourself to
make anything happen and for what you
want to come true.

Napoleon Hill, in the well-known book
Think and Grow Rich, says that whatever
we desire we are capable of achieving.

I believe we are programmed to desire
what we are meant to do with our precious
life. I believe that every single person
makes a contribution to society, which is
necessary for the world to function. It's a
beautiful thing.

Most of us don't realize that our lives are
meant to be great. We are meant to be
happy. We are meant to live fulfilling lives.
Because the happier we are the better

people we become to each other, which makes us even better.

How do you feel when someone treats you well compared to when someone treats you badly? How do you feel when you act well toward others verses when you act badly toward others? When we act good we feel good, when we act bad we feel bad.

The more fulfilled people are, the happier they are, which makes them better contributors to society. We are programmed to desire what we are meant to do and when we fulfill that desire, our natural emotion is happiness.

To fulfill your desire, you must believe you CAN do whatever you want to do. Imagine having no desire to exercise. Do you think you could exercise? What if you had the desire to exercise? Do you think you could?

Here are three ways to create powerful belief within yourself. These are the techniques that helped me up those hills on my bike and on the tough hills of life that I climbed to gain confidence in myself.

Most of my life I had little belief that I could do the things I wanted to do. After much research, learning and listening to my own voice, I began to believe I could do anything I desired to do.

The three most powerful tools that I have found to help create belief in yourself are:
1. Doing Something
2. Positive Self Talk
3. Visualization

Doing Something
Doing something can give you confidence. The more you do something, the more

confident you become at doing it and the more you believe in yourself.

When I decided to go on that bike trip I didn't feel up to the challenge. But, I went anyway. After making it all the way to the top of the first hill I began to believe in myself. I began to believe I could make it through the whole trip.

In the end it was one of the best trips I've ever been on. If I hadn't gone, I never would have felt so good about myself and never would have had all that FUN.

Think back to a time when you didn't believe you could do something, but did it anyway. Your confidence increased.

Maybe you didn't think you could play a song on the piano. After you did it, you felt more confident about playing the piano. Maybe you did something at work, or took a job you didn't think you could do. Maybe you started playing a sport, or started an exercise program. When your confidence increases you begin to believe that you can achieve.

I have a relative who would never pick up a tennis racket and attempt a swing. She said that she was too uncoordinated. One day, we dragged her onto the court, handed her a racket, and forced her to play. We needed a fourth for doubles and she was the only one around.

We had tried to get her on the courts for over ten years and we had finally succeeded. We taught her what to do, and she did it. She swung, and even hit a couple of balls over the net. When it was time for us to go, we couldn't get her off the court. She loved playing so much, she didn't want to stop.

That week, she bought a tennis racket, joined a tennis club, and began taking lessons. She fell in love with the sport. Later I asked her why she thought she was uncoordinated. I asked if anyone used to tell her when she was a kid that she was uncoordinated. She answered, "Yes, all the time."

Negative Comments and Influences

Many of us have negative comments directed at us all our lives. Things like, "you will always be fat" or "you will never be successful".

We must erase all the negative comments we have ever heard and are still hearing. They don't get us anywhere, and they aren't true. They are only someone's opinion.

The most successful people in the world do what they love to do. They don't listen to negative comments that will keep them from accomplishing their personal and professional goals.

Disconnect from the opinions that contribute to your unhappiness.

These opinions are probably the ones of your loved ones. Maybe you still hear the voices and opinions of your parents, teachers and siblings in your own head. Know that they are or were wonderful people who wanted the best for you and only did what they knew. You may think the way they showed you love was not love at all, but they may see it as the only way they knew how to show love because that is how it was shown to them. They are wonderful people who love you, and everything they have ever done was in your best interest. They are just individuals with their limiting beliefs about themselves and others. They only know what their parents and the society in which they lived taught them.

Sometimes people who can't see something for themselves, have a difficult time being able to see it for others. For example, if you say to a friend, "I've decided to learn how to sky dive" they may reply, "You'll never be able to go through with it. Besides, why do you even want to do something so crazy?"

This conversation might discourage you from going ahead with your plans. Do you give others more credibility about what you want and desire than you give yourself? You decide they're right. But the truth is, whatever you desire, you are capable of achieving.

Take a minute now to think about a time you wanted to do something, but someone discouraged you from doing it. How did you feel? Maybe you felt deprived, empty, or depressed.

Now, take a minute to think of a time you did something you wanted to do, despite any negative input you received. Think of a time you didn't allow anyone to keep you from doing that one thing.

For me, it was a vacation, a job, and a dating relationship. Each time I didn't listen to others. I listened to myself and experienced the best vacation I ever had, the best job I ever had, and the best relationship I ever had.

What worked for me, was deciding ahead of time, before I told anyone about my plan, I wasn't going to allow negative input to affect me. To prepare myself for negativity, I needed to realize how much I wanted what I wanted and how much happiness and fulfillment it would bring me.

I needed to talk to myself in a positive and powerful way. I needed to build my confidence. I needed to have confidence that my decisions were the right ones. I needed to give myself more credibility than I gave others.

If you want to build your confidence, and I know you do because you are reading this book, use the techniques in these chapters, and watch your confidence sky rocket.

Positive Self Talk

Be your own best friend.

Do you like it when others say things like, "You're stupid for doing that," "You should lose some weight", "You will never be successful" or "You aren't very smart"? Well... if you don't like it when others say those things to you, why do you say them to yourself? Don't pretend that you don't. Everyone does. At one time or another you have said things to yourself like, "I'm so fat," "I'm not as good as they are," "I can't do it," "I was stupid for doing that." What we tell ourselves is what we become.

FROM THIS DAY FORWARD MAKE A VOW TO YOURSELF TO ONLY SPEAK POSITIVELY TO YOURSELF.

For years I tried to lose weight, while I kept telling myself how fat I was. What happened? I gained, and gained, and gained. I now work hard at telling myself how thin and fit I am. Sure I forget sometimes and go back to my old habits of saying how fat I am. That will be a challenge for you too, falling back into old habits of negative self talk. Be aware when it happens, catch yourself, and change it to positive self talk immediately.

Whatever you want to become, talk to yourself as if it is already true. If you want a promotion in your company, treat yourself as if you already have that promotion. If you want to lose weight, treat yourself as if you are already at your ideal weight, if you want to have more friends, treat yourself as if you have many friends. Become your own best friend rather than your own worst critic. Whatever you tell yourself, your subconscious mind takes seriously and stores away.

Most of us are waiting for validation from others. We're waiting for someone else to say, "You can get that promotion." "You are smart." "You are sexy." "You're very likeable." Most people shoot you down, rather than build you up. You end up with lower self-confidence than before.

But you keep waiting for what you want to hear. Stop waiting, and tell yourself what you want to hear. Give yourself more credit than others give you. You know more about yourself anyway. After all, you are with yourself 24-hours a day. Don't you know yourself better than anyone else knows you?

If you don't think so, you lack self-confidence. If you think you can run your own business, but everyone around you is saying you can't, most likely, you are right and they are wrong.

Trust yourself. Don't rely on others to build up your confidence. Build your own confidence. It's your opinion of yourself that matters most. Get in the habit of positive self talk: "I am smart. I am wonderful. I am sexy. I am beautiful. I am active. I am fun to be around." Whatever you tell yourself and believe about yourself, you will become.

When I decided to enter the training & development field, I knew it was what I really wanted to do, but I felt the need to convince myself I could do it. I had never been a trainer before, and I was applying for training positions. First I needed to convince myself that I could be an excellent trainer, and could actually get hired. If I couldn't convince myself, how could I convince the person interviewing me?

I wrote in my journal every day, over and over again "I am a trainer. I have the skills to be a trainer. I am an excellent trainer." On my way to my first interview, I said out loud in the car, "I am a trainer, I am a trainer, I am a trainer, I am an excellent trainer, I am an excellent trainer, I am an excellent trainer, I will get this job I will get this job, and I will get this job!" I repeated it over and over and over again for the entire 45 minute ride.

I was hired on the spot. It didn't stop there. After one week of training on the job, the feedback I was getting was extraordinary. People were telling me that I was an excellent trainer.

Writing Exercise - **Positive Thoughts**

Do this writing exercise. Think about one thing that you would like to convince yourself you can do or be. Write it over and over again. At least seven times, but if you could write it over and over for more than 10 minutes, that would be even better.

Write down what you want to believe about yourself, what you would like to hear from others around you and the type of person that you would like to be. Write in the present tense.

Examples: *I am intelligent. I have lots of energy. I am a leader. I am a patient and tolerant person. I am fun to be with. I am sexy. I am an entrepreneur. I am excellent at my job. I am gorgeous!*

This is a very powerful exercise. Write in your journal and talk to yourself in this manner all day long.

Have you ever had a hair cut when you thought it looked awful? Then a friend tells you it looks great and you reply, "No it doesn't; it looks awful." But they continue to tell you how great it looks. Eventually you begin to believe them. You finally begin to think that maybe it does look great.

The same thing happens from what you repeat to yourself. If you want to believe something about yourself, tell it to yourself over and over again, until you do believe it.

Visualization

In my workshops I ask people what is the one thing that is stopping them from achieving what they want. The answer is almost always lack of self-confidence. It is amazing to me how many people in our country lack self-confidence. The sad thing is that self-confidence is the most important thing you need to succeed.

Here are helpful techniques designed to increase your confidence and to create belief within yourself that you can have whatever you want.

Take a minute now and imagine that you have total self-confidence. Imagine yourself with more confidence than anyone at your place of work. Imagine yourself with more confidence than anyone in your family. Imagine yourself with more confidence than anyone else that is interviewing for the same job you are. Imagine yourself with more confidence than any of your friends. Imagine yourself with more confidence than anyone in the world. That's right, the world. After spending a few seconds with your eyes closed imaging yourself with total self-confidence, write the answers to the following questions.

What did you see when you closed your eyes? What were you doing? How were you acting? If you believed that you could achieve anything you wanted to achieve, how would your life be different? What would you do?

Go back to the writing exercise in Chapter 4 called **Zapped**, in which you wrote about your dream life in the present tense. Read what you wrote, and then answer the following question: If you had total confidence and total belief within yourself that you could have this (what you wrote in zapped exercise) would you go after it?

Close your eyes and visualize yourself living your dream. Do this now.

Our potential is unlimited. We can go as far as we want, but we must be able to see ourselves the way we want to be in order to become what we want to be.

You can have whatever you wrote down. However, you will probably have to work hard to get it.

You might say, "Well I don't want to work hard." Who does? Look at your life right now. I bet you are already working hard at something you don't even enjoy. Why not work hard at something that will be fun and rewarding? When you are growing and improving your life, you are happier, you have more energy, and lots more fun. When you feel good, your self-confidence increases.

The hard work is reconditioning and re-programming your brain. Breaking the habits that don't get you what you want, and creating new habits that will get you what you do want. Change the way you think and your life will change.

It is said, "If you always think what you've always thought, you'll always get what you've always got." If you keep doing the same thing over and over you will always get the same results. To get different results, you must do something different.

Now you may be saying, "But this is who I am. I don't want to lose ME." First of all, you can't lose who you really are. Secondly, if part of who you are right now isn't making you happy or if it's not giving you freedom, fun, and fulfillment, why not lose that part of you? What have you got to lose? Or, rather, what have you got to gain?

A few years ago, I was out to dinner with a friend. I was starting to come out of my rut and take control of my life. I was taking the steps I am sharing with you in this book. I remember saying to her. "The old Jacki is coming back." She said something that I will never forget. She said, "It's not the old Jacki, it's the new and improved Jacki." Wow "new and improved!" That means even MORE than what the old Jacki was.

This idea gave me even more energy and motivation to go after what I wanted in life. If you think you would like to be the way you were, forget it! Focus on becoming the *new and improved* you! Better than you've ever been.

A flower may have the potential to grow to a certain height, but without water it will stop growing, and wilt, or stop growing altogether. When it rains or someone waters it, miraculously it comes back to life and grows even taller. It doesn't revert to where it was; it gets even better. It is still the same flower, but new and improved.

We are always growing older but if we want we can grow bigger, better, and stronger. If you want to become new and improved, better than you ever have been; remember we're all like the flowers. Even when you get into a rut, you can turn your life around and grow bigger, better, and stronger. All you need is the right nourishment, which is the belief that you deserve and are meant to live a happy and fulfilling life.

Your future is so bright
You will need sunglasses!

Susan Evans

Chapter 6

GO FOR IT

Step 3
Take Action and Make It Happen

You now know how to discover what you really want. You now know how to create belief within yourself that you can have what you really want. Now it's time to learn how to make it happen. If you don't think you can have it, you won't even try.

When I'm bicycling with a group of people and a few really fast riders pass me, I don't even try to catch up to them because I know I can't. But, sometimes I notice myself going faster than I thought I could. If a faster rider passes me, I ride a little faster. I notice that I'm not losing him or her so quickly so I begin riding even faster. When I believe I can keep up, I work harder and faster. When I don't believe I can keep up, I usually slow down and go at a slower pace and don't even try to go faster.

Once you believe that you can achieve your goals, motivation comes naturally. Motivation comes from believing in yourself. Aren't you more motivated to go after something that you know you can get? Here are four ways to help you take action and stay motivated.

1. Take control of your life
2. Take small steps
3. Gain energy
4. Act the part

Take Control of Your Life
You are the only one who has control over your life. It's important that you realize that. Too many of us don't realize the internal power we have over our own lives.

We don't realize that if we are miserable, overweight, or haven't achieved what we want, that it's our own doing. We tend to blame others by saying, "If only my family, friends, and supervisors treated me differently, my life would be so much better."

Your first action step is to take control of your life. Look within to your internal power and potential. Once you believe you have the power, you will be able to take control. When you know what you want and believe you can have it, you will be much more successful in taking control of your life.

Tell yourself that you are in control. Every waking hour and non-waking hour, say to yourself, "I am in total control of my life and myself." By now you know the benefits of positive self talk. Say something enough times to yourself, and eventually your conscious and subconscious mind will believe it and will work toward getting it.

Write Down What You Want

Be specific. Don't say, "I want to find a job I love." Write down what that job is. If you want to make a lot of money, write down exactly how much money. The more specific you can be the better.
Studies have shown that people who write their goals are much more likely to achieve them. Writing helps get the message to your subconscious mind. It helps you organize your thoughts and it helps you to commit to them. Write ideas down.

Once you have written down what you want, brainstorm with yourself for ways to achieve that goal. Find a quiet spot, give yourself some time, and ask yourself the question, "How can I achieve this goal." Then, write down everything that enters your mind. Whether you think it's possible or not, whether you think it's something you would or could do, just write it down.

Yes – this is very similar to the writing exercise you did to discover what you want. After you have twenty ideas, circle your top ten. Then circle the top five from that ten, then the top three. Then put a star next to your #1 favorite item. Begin by taking action on that one item.

Small Steps

When you begin taking action steps, start small. Small actions will grow into something bigger. Just as a plant grows, it begins with a seed. That seed grows slowly, and when we take care of it and nurture it, it gets bigger and bigger. When we encourage it to keep growing, it does.

Does someone who plans to run a marathon have to be in shape before they start training? Of course not, they can begin by walking, then running a little. Gradually they add more and more mileage to their workouts. They start very small, and eventually accomplish something very big — running 26.2 miles!

Everything you do is like a marathon. Start small and gradually do a little more that will move you closer to your goal. You will eventually accomplish what you want. It will feel like you have completed a marathon.

Before I discovered my passion for public speaking, I had no idea what I wanted to do with my life. While I was out of work, with no idea what I wanted my next career to be, I operated a singles club.

At times I had to speak to groups at singles events. I was so nervous that my heart pounded and I couldn't see straight or remember what I had said. I decided to try to get over my nervousness and fear by joining Toastmasters.

After giving my very first Toastmasters speech, my confidence began to increase. I had more energy, and I was motivated to write my next speech. This in turn led to completing the ten-speech manual within a year.

I noticed that almost every speech I gave was inspirational or motivational. Eventually I discovered my true passion of motivational speaking. This led to giving speeches in public, which led to a speaking business, which led to writing and publishing this book.

Reading books on public speaking motivated and inspired me to keep going and learn more. Surrounding yourself with people and things associated with what you want motivates you to keep going, take more action, and get what you really want.

Find people, groups, associations, books, activities, lectures, seminars and classes related to what you want or think you want. In addition to gaining knowledge, you will be motivated and inspired to take action and work toward what you want.

When your life is moving in the direction you want it to go, you gradually make progress, and you enjoy that progress each step of the way. This is what creates a happy and fulfilling life.

Begin setting small goals. Each time you accomplish a small goal you will tend to make the next goal a little bit bigger, and so on. Think of a ladder. Isn't it easier to take one rung at a time, rather than skipping over a couple of steps? When you climb step by step, you get to the top more easily and in much better condition. It is much easier than trying to jump to the top rung or skip steps.

Gain Energy

To go after what you want you need to have energy. You get energy by moving your body in a fun way. Your body is meant to move!

Every living thing on this planet moves in order to survive. Have you ever seen a squirrel take a bus, a bird fly a plane, or a fish row a boat. Humans are the only living things that do not move their bodies, as they were intended to move.

To survive, we need to move. This does not necessarily mean going to the gym, taking aerobics, and working out with weights, although those are very good things to do. It means doing what you enjoy.

What is fun for you? Do you like being outside in the fresh air? If so, go for a walk, a hike or a bike ride. If you like the water, row a boat, take up sailing, or canoe down the river. Do you like to garden, to dance, to play with the dog, with the kids or the grand kids? You get the picture.

When you move your body in a fun way, your energy increases and you have FUN! When you have fun, not only do you have more energy, but you get happier. When you are happy, you are more productive and when you are more productive you can accomplish what you want and become who you want to become.

When we are happy we are better people. We treat others better and we set a great example for others. Many people spread negativity. Happiness can be spread just as easily. When you have fun, you automatically become happier. Some may consider this being selfish. On the contrary, it is selfish not to have fun. Then you are not as happy and productive and can't influence others in a positive way. The more fun you have, the better person you will become to others.

You must be happy if you want to help others be happy too. Be happy and you will be a better contributor to your loved ones and to society.

Act The Part

This is one of my favorite steps. I find this technique makes me feel really good about myself. It also helps me create the person I am meant to be and want to be. It will do the same for you too!

Act the part you want to be. Act as if you already have what you want. If you want a million dollars, walk around as if you already have a million dollars.

What would you do? Who would you hang out with? Where would you go? How would you feel? The more you act the way you want to be, the more you will feel it and the more likely you will get it.

Find people who already have what you want. Talk to them, watch them, and do what they do. Use positive self-talk. It will train your subconscious mind to attract what you are meant to have. Tell yourself that you deserve to have what you are meant to have. You deserve to have it all. You are meant to live a life of freedom, fun, and fulfillment!

Chapter 7

What I learned from
The Wizard of Oz

"We're off to see the wizard, the wonderful wizard of Oz... because, because, because, because. Because of the wonderful things he does."

The Wizard of Oz is one of the greatest movies of all time. I loved it when I was a kid, but as an adult I relate to it so much more. The movie is about a girl who goes on a journey to get what she wants, to go home. Along the way she meets three friends who also have a burning desire to get what they want — a brain, a heart, and some courage.

They journey down the yellow brick road together to go after what they want. Along the way they have setbacks. There are obstacles they must overcome. There are attack trees, a wicked witch, and the poppies. Each time, they picked themselves up and continued to the City of Oz where all their dreams would come true.

I have taken my own journey down my own yellow brick road. A journey of learning how to get what I want out of life. A journey in which I discovered who was the greatest influence in my life. Each time I listened to myself, I experienced wonderful things — the best vacation I've ever had, the best relationship I've ever had, and the best job I've ever had.

What were your best vacation, your best relationship, and your best job? Who influenced you? Did you do those things because someone told you that you should, or did you do them because you knew they would make you happy?

In order for me to get what I wanted the greatest influence in my life had to be ME. Once I made a conscious choice to be my only influence and not let anyone keep me from getting what I wanted, I was able to experience joy, excitement, and fulfillment in my life.

For many years I was influenced by the most important people in my life, which were my parents, family, and friends. They loved me and wanted the best for me. But these are the same people who actually talked me out of vacations I wanted to take, men I wanted to date, and careers I wanted to pursue. They all had convincing arguments about why I shouldn't pursue the things I wanted.

I allowed their influence to be more powerful than my own desires. I believed they were right and that I was wrong. They believed they were giving me the best advice. But, listening to them, instead of myself, resulted in a very unfulfilling life.

Whatever you desire you are capable of achieving. How many people told the New England Patriots they couldn't make it to the Super bowl? Did they listen? No! They said: "Don't talk to me." They had desire, they had a goal, and they believed they could do it. They did it by being their own greatest influence.

If you want to be fulfilled, if you want to be happy, if you want to live an exciting life, you must — I repeat, you must — believe in yourself! Do not wait for someone else to believe in you. They will believe in you after you believe in yourself. When you believe in yourself, you will accomplish what you want. Then people have no choice but to believe in you. We teach people how to treat us. Everyone now believes in the Patriots, don't they?

When you believe in yourself, you accomplish what you want. When you accomplish what you want you become happy and fulfilled. When you are happy and fulfilled you become a better person; a better parent, a better spouse, a better employee, a better boss, a better friend.

Several years ago, I had no life. I was out of work, and I didn't know what I wanted. I desperately wanted more out of life, but I wasn't getting more because I didn't believe in myself. I was waiting for others to believe in me. That wasn't happening.

I listened to others, instead of myself. When I allowed other people's influence to be more powerful than my own desires, I became unfulfilled and depressed.

I took the journey down the yellow brick road to discover the power to get what I wanted, to become my only influence and to believe in myself. Today, I am the happiest and most fulfilled I have ever been because I know what I want and I know where I'm going. I'm enjoying the process of getting there and enjoying my accomplishments and progress.

Like the characters in the Wizard of Oz, I run into obstacles. But each time I pick myself up and continue on.

You too will run into obstacles, and probably already have many times. This is normal. It is all part of life and creating the life you want. Just remember that obstacles only slow you down a little bit. Simply pick yourself up and continue on.

Be your own positive influence and focus on your destination.

Listen to yourself. Know that what you want is already inside of you. It may be buried deep underneath other people's influences, negative self-talk, and lack of confidence, but it is there.

At the end of the movie, the Scarecrow, Tin Man, Lion, and Dorothy realized that no one could give them what they wanted. Not even the great and powerful Wizard of Oz. Only they had that power. Best of all, they had that power all along.

When they realized they had the power, they all got what they wanted. When the Scarecrow realized his ability to think, he got his brain. When the Tin Man realized his ability to feel, he got his heart. When the Lion realized his ability to be brave, he got his courage. When they discovered their abilities and their power, they were able to get what they wanted almost immediately.

Once Dorothy realized she had the power to go home, it only took her three clicks.

All of you have had the power all along. Once you discover your power, once you believe in yourself, and once you become your only influence, you will be able to achieve your greatest desires.

And just like Dorothy, you too may get what you want in only three clicks.

Conclusion

It is my belief that we were all created with a purpose and that every person is programmed to know what they can contribute here on earth. We are programmed to desire what we are meant to achieve. When we carry out our purpose we are happy and fulfilled. When we are happy and fulfilled, we are better people and better contributors to society.

The happier you are the happier people around you will be. If you don't want to be selfish, then you must live out your dreams. Not living out your dreams, being unhappy and unfulfilled is really being selfish. No matter who you are, you affect those around you. When you live out your dreams you teach others how to be their best and how to make a greater contribution to society.

This doesn't mean you have to become a super hero or have a super job. It means doing what you derive pleasure from. If you want to be a wonderful parent, then that is your purpose in life. If you want to be a landscaper, then that is what you are meant to do. If you desire to be an artist, an entertainer, or a big executive, then that is what you are meant to do. Listen to yourself. Be your only influence.

To get what you want out of life, you must believe in yourself and have control over your own life. Too many of us have allowed others to run our lives. Their thoughts, their beliefs, and their opinions direct us.

Many of us have had trouble developing our own opinions. We have trouble believing our opinions are right.

Here are the stories of two people I know. One has no belief in herself. She has no control over her life. The other used to lack control, but now knows how to exert control over his life.

Julie has no control over her life. Therefore, her life is out of control. She has allowed her parents and ex-husband to control her. She allows her kids to control her. She never learned how to take control of her own life so her self-esteem is very low.

She relies on her parents for financial support as well as for day care. She feels she must cater to everyone except herself. She does not believe in herself. Because of this she doesn't take good care of herself either. She's at least 100 pounds overweight, doesn't exercise and never gets enough sleep. She's unhappy in her job, but won't look for another one because she doesn't have enough self-confidence to think that she could get another job.

How sad is that? This is a girl who is remarkably intelligent and has many talents. I told her many times that I see incredible potential in her, but she doesn't see it in herself.

We become however we see ourselves. To become anything greater, we must change our perception of ourselves.

My friend Jim believes in himself, and he is going places. For many years, like many gay people, he struggled for self-acceptance. When he finally accepted himself, he began living his life the way it was meant to be lived.

It was hard for his family when he told them he was gay. But he believed in himself and accepted himself. He knew he was a good person and he believed he was okay. Because of his belief in himself, he was able to deal with his family's negative reaction and create a happy, healthy and fulfilling life for himself. Jim didn't always have belief in himself. He did the work that was necessary to be done in order to feel better on the inside so he could have a great life on the outside.

Take control of your life. You only have one. Why not make it the best it can be? You deserve to have whatever you want. But only you can make it happen.

Some of us need convincing. Use the tools provided in this book to help you discover what you want, create belief within yourself that you can have it, and to gain the energy and motivation to take action and make it happen.

You have the ability to gain the confidence you need to succeed.

You have the ability to create freedom, fun and fulfillment in your life.

You have the ability to go out and find something greater out there for you.

TAKE YOUR LIFE AND LOVE IT!

Other books by Jacki Rose

11 Steps to Powerful Public Speaking

Take the Stage & Love It

100 Public Speaking Tips

Fear to Fabulous Presentation Workbook Guide

www.JackiRose.com